Maximize Your Investments!

How to Achieve the Most Profit with the Least Capital

By: Betty Wright

9781635014952

I0510813

PUBLISHERS NOTES

Disclaimer – Speedy Publishing LLC

Speedy Publishing LLC

40 E Main Street, Newark, Delaware, 19711

Contact Us: 1-888-248-4521

Website: http://www.speedypublishing.co

REPRINTED Paperback Edition: 9781635014952:

Manufactured in the United States of America

DEDICATION

This book is dedicated to my husband, James. You are a fighter. We will always remember you as a strong father and husband.

TABLE OF CONTENTS

Chapter 1- The Idea Behind and Uses of the Profit Tunnel 5

Chapter 2- Tested Strategies That Bring in the Cash 10

Chapter 3- What Profit Strategy Should You Employ? 24

Chapter 4- Boost Sales with Quality Information 29

Chapter 5- Using Web SEO 32

Chapter 6- The Killer Offer and the Resulting Mailing List 37

Chapter 7- How to Keep List Building a Legal Tactic 42

About The Author 52

CHAPTER 1- THE IDEA BEHIND AND USES OF THE PROFIT TUNNEL

Nothing warms the cockles of a salesperson more than getting a new client. Often you are able to secure that new client because you have a quality core good or service that is provided at a competitive price.

While you may not make a great deal off that initial offering, there will no doubt be the chance to build on your initial rapport with your new client and engage in the task many sales people know as "up-selling."

That is where the concept of the Profit Tunnel comes into play.

Maximize Your Investments!

The Profit Tunnel is your pathway to building a relationship with your customer that begins with the purchase of initial goods or services. Once that initial relationship is established, you build on that relationship by evaluating the needs of your client and identify other goods or services that will also benefit your customer.

As you are able to acquaint, interest, and finally sell additional and often higher priced items to your customer, your profit margin will increase. The Profit Tunnel model works very well whether you are working with a brick and mortar business or going strictly with an online presence.

In both instances, the task involves winning the confidence of the prospect, identifying entry level products or services that will be of interest to the prospect, selling the prospect on the goods or services, and then continuing to offer additional products or enhancements that will make life even easier for that former prospect that is now your customer.

Low Ticket

When it comes to winning the confidence of a prospect, nothing speaks louder than a good deal. Persons who are responsible for securing goods and services for their employer love to save the company money.

It enhances his or her reputation with the officers and owners. At the same time, no one wants to end up with a low cost service that ends up being a dud. This means the good or service needs to perform well along with being cost efficient.

Your job is to match low cost quality goods or services with the business type of your prospect. Once you demonstrate how one of your low cost offerings will consistently outperform the competition and save money for the prospect's employer, you will be poised to help roll out your low cost offering throughout the organization, making your profit in volume distribution initially.

Once your offering is functioning throughout the organization, you may find that not only do you have the ear of your initial contact, but now you have the ability to interact with persons throughout the organization that may be interested in other offerings that you can supply.

Providing additional goods or services that are in a similar price range will be another way you will increase the profit margin. This is sometimes referred to as lateral selling.

Simply put, you are not really pushing items with a higher price tag, or even enhancements to services you have already sold which would increase the profits. You are simply broadening your current situation to include more of the same, from a charge perspective.

There is nothing wrong with lateral selling. In fact, it can be quite profitable. However, in time it reaches a point where there is no more room for more of the same and you need to move on to the next level.

Mid Ticket

Now safely ensconced with several low cost offerings, you can begin to look at other needs of your customer. Chances are you have goods or services that may be used on a less frequent basis, but carry a higher price tag.

With your low cost items working just fine for your client, you will easily be able to gain attention for these mid-priced offerings.

Maximize Your Investments!

As part of your presentation, it is important to demonstrate not only what you have to offer today, but also be prepared to present the attributes of the offering in such a way that your client can begin to brainstorm possibly uses within the organization.

You may want to have one or two ideas ready, just to prime the thinking process, if necessary. But the more your client can come up with possible uses, the greater his ownership of using the mid ticket item will become, and the closer you will be to another sale.

Be prepared to have to wait until the timing is right to spring your mid ticket item on your client. If the item is only going to be used a few times a year, the interest level may not be there until the time is growing near for the next relevant event.

By all means introduce the item but if your client wants to put off the discussion until closer to time, lock in a date and time to renew the discussions.

High Ticket – Extremely High Ticket

The dream of selling high ticket good or services is often the goal of the salesperson. After all, who would not love to be able to sell five thousand dollar items in one afternoon, rather than spend the entire week selling hundred dollar items in order to make the same commission?

Of course, you want to be on the alert for any chance to introduce and sell a high ticket item.

You have a couple of things going for you at this point in your relationship with your client.

First, there is the matter of the proven track record of the low ticket and mid ticket offerings they have already tried and found to be great for their business operations. Nothing breeds confidence in a supplier the way that an ongoing record of excellence will.

Second, you have demonstrated a continual desire to bring their attention to goods or services that have relevance to the business. You are not laying your entire product line out on the table and asking them to figure out what they need. You are someone who does the legwork first and then brings items to their attention. That you care enough to understand their business and do some legwork on their behalf says a lot about your integrity.

What his means for you is that when you call your contact about arranging a demonstration of a high ticket item, you are already more than halfway to making a sale. The attitude will not be "prove this is worth my time," but "let's find out how we can use this."

When you go into a live or virtual demonstration with your client working with that type of mindset, your chances of closing the sale are very high indeed.

The Profit Tunnel helps you understand that your relationship with your client works on several levels and in several phases.

Building upon the sterling reputation you establish with low ticket sales and rolling it into the sale of more profitable sales will not only ensure you a great commission, but also will provide you with a working relationship that will last for many years.

CHAPTER 2- TESTED STRATEGIES THAT BRING IN THE CASH

Low Ticket Product Ideas

When you think in terms of low ticket products or services, you are talking about items that usually carry no more than a $27.00 price tag. The most common average range for a low ticket item would be in the $5.00 to $9.95 range.

There are many of online and brick and mortar businesses that consider low ticket items to be the bread and butter of the business, the way that you keep the lights on every month.

Of course, in order for those low ticket items to keep a steady flow of basic revenue, there is the need to promote your offerings and entice new clients to give them a try. Here are a few ideas that may help you promote your low ticket offerings to fresh faces.

• **Special Reports**

Spotlighting the low ticket items that are your biggest sellers to a wide range of customer demographics is a great way to get the attention of prospects.

A special report is going to essentially focus on two things: first, this is a product or service that has is being successfully used by hundreds of thousands of people right this very minute.

Second, this product or service can make a big impact in the quality of your life and work. Once you have it, you will not understand how you ever got along without it.

These types of special report promotions are meant to spotlight all the positive attributes of your offering. You want to talk about the great performance, the low maintenance, and of course the low price.

One thing that can help dress up a special report is charts and relevant graphics. Most people are visual in the way they relate to the world, so using a simple chart to illustrate a point, or inserting some other type of visual that is related to the subject matter will help to enhance and hold the attention of the reader.

Testimonials from current clients also are a big part of a successful special report. If at all possible, vary the industry types that are represented in your testimonials.

Maximize Your Investments!

The broader the use of your offering in various parts of the business world, the more likely a prospect is to see the need to investigate a little more closely.

Special reports are relatively easy to produce and extremely cost effective to have available. The content can be used in a direct mail piece that can be reproduced cheaply.

The special report can be posted online, with a unique URL that can then be distributed far and wide by both manual and electronic means. The result is an effective promotional tool that has a very lost cost to create and has the potential to yield big returns in a very short time.

• Short Audio Sessions

Have you ever listened to those short audio clips that are on many web sites? They often are informative and can spur people to look more closely at a product or service.

Short audio sessions are not anything new. For decades, businesses have employed fifteen-second audio sessions to promote their products while callers were on hold, waiting to speak with a customer service rep.

Theater owners have employed them to get in a plug for concessions that are sold in the theater lobby. Who among us have not heard a short audio session while in the grocery store or in a discount retail store?

Given the history of the success of short audio sessions, it is no wonder that they are also working on the Internet as well.

To a degree, a short audio session makes the sales process via the Internet a little more personal, as the prospect hears a human voice. That alone makes the session an appealing way to reach a certain part of the populace.

Of course, a successful short audio session is going to be to the point and informative. It will give the prospect enough to ensure he or she will progress to the next level and seriously consider the offering, rather than simply scanning some text and moving on to another web site.

Settle on the subject for the session, make is crisp, clear, and easy to understand. Then shut up before you get too wordy.

- **Trial Membership Offers**

Everybody wants to get a bargain, but there are those that will sit on the fence forever before making a decision. A trial membership offer can be just what you need to get them to commit.

There are several things that are very attractive to a prospect. Among them are:

- There is no long-term commitment. If I don't like what I see during the trial period, I simply move on.

- I don't have to pay full price. Most trial offers will be at a discount, so very little revenue is invested.

- The trial offer gives me the chance to test drive and show the offering to other people who would be using it. I can find out up front if they see any advantages to using this new offering

- This gives me the chance to think of questions that should be answered before a commitment is made. I may think of something while in the trial period that I would not think of during a simple demonstration.

If you offer a trial membership, make sure you provided specific terms, as well as a way for the prospect to convert the trial membership into a full membership at any time during the trial.

- **Trial Software Offers**

If software is involved in your product or service offering, you may also want to provide a demonstration version of the software that is good for a limited amount of time. Think in terms of some of the free electronic trail games you can download.

Many of them will allow the player to access and start a new game session for a specific number of times before the software becomes inoperative and they player will have to purchase the full version in order to continue.

Trial software should be representative of what the full version does, but you want to make sure that the software cannot be reconfigured to get around the limited time usage.

This is not a difficult task for anyone who develops software; all you will need to do is provide the perimeters of the trial time and you are all set.

As with the trial membership offers, you want your prospect to be able to upgrade from trial to permanent software at any point during the trial time, so make sure you include that in your package as well.

Promoting your low ticket items will keep your company moving along, providing the operating capital that you need to enhance your offerings and also develop more high priced offerings as well.

By utilizing these and similar ideas, you can effectively increase your client base without investing a huge chunk of your profits into public relations endeavors.

Mid Ticket Product Ideas

Having established yourself with some of your low ticket offerings, you will want to investigate the potential for up-selling your client by creating interest in your mid ticket products and services.

For the purposes of the discussion, you may want to think of mid ticket items as being priced in the $37.00 to $67.00 range per unit.

There are plenty of methods you can use to promote your mid ticket offerings. Here are some examples of methods that have proven track records of generating interest among existing clientele as well as garnering some attention from new customers as well.

• **E-Books**

It seems that no matter what the type of product or service that is offered, an electronic book will be an ideal way to generate interest. Why? There are actually several levels on which an E-book attracts us. Here are three examples:

• In spite of the hype, most of us do like to read. We will read everything from sonnets to the backs of cereal boxes.

- E-books are easily stored. We can download them onto our hard drives and read them any time we like.

- E-books are often free or available at a fraction of the cost of a hard copy book.

When using an E-book to promote your product line, you will most likely have it available as a free download.

Providing a few online excerpts from the book as "hooks" will entice people to take the few moments needed to download the book and will also increase the chances they will actually read it after downloading.

You may want to also give them the chance to read a few pages before they perform a download, assuming you have the bandwidth required for this sort of activity.

Another potential way to keep the relationship going is to have a sign-up page where basic contact information is collected before the download commences.

This will give you the chance to follow up on everyone that downloaded the book and perhaps close a sale very quickly, due to the obvious fact of your diligence.

- **Paid Membership Sites**

When you run a paid membership site, one of the things you must do in order to maintain and grow your client base is provide something that makes people feel like that monthly membership fee they pay is worth the cost.

As an example, you may include a short weekly or monthly newsletter as one of the perks of being a member of the site. Don't fill it with mindless fluff that circulates around the Internet constantly.

Make the information relevant to your customers, to your product line and most of all worth the time to read about. Use it to talk about upcoming enhancements to favorite products, do a spotlight on one of your customers and the work he or she does.

Along with the newsletter, make sure there is access to online pages that capture the attention of your customers. Perhaps you can arrange for them to download a coupon they can use locally as part of a promotion campaign.

You may supply a message board where clients can talk about how they employ the goods or services you sell. The point is to make the membership perks something that people will want to engage in often enough that they want to maintain access to those perks.

- **Software / Scripts**

Software that fills a need with your customers can be a great thing. Depending on where you draw your majority of clients from, this can be just about anything from software that helps to catalog plants to software that helps to design a home accounting systems, to software that can be used to track sales efforts.

In short, you identify and anticipate needs within your client base and then come up with the software that will meet those needs.

Now, do you develop proprietary software or do you partner with someone and act as an agent for that partner? It all depends. If you can entering into an agreement that allows you to make a decent profit from the sale of the software and still offer it to your clientele at a price that is better than what they can get it for themselves, the answer is yes.

If you can barely get a better deal than standard retail, forget it and try to develop your own software products. If the profit is not there for you, and the savings is not there for your clients, then the project is of no value to either of you.

Keep in mind the software can cover just about any subject you want. For development ideas, why not query your current clients?

Ask them what type of software they would like to see, and what types of bells and whistles would be attractive to them. You may be surprised at how easily you can fulfill those wishes.

Audio/Video Sessions

Once upon a time, companies trained new people at large gatherings. These days, new employees attend audio and web conferences via the Internet, saving time and money to all concerned.

Audio and video sessions have applications in all sorts of ways. Did you know that there are churches that conduct Sunday school classes with audio and video links, so that members who are unable to get to the actual church can attend and participate?

One a denominational level, there is a denomination headquartered in the Mid-West that broadcasts both worship and business sessions of its bi-annual denominational conference to members all over the world, via live feed and data streaming.

Audio/video sessions using the Internet can revolve around all sorts of subjects, from how to fix a flat tire to detailed sessions on fixing broken relationships. They can include travelogues to exotic and distant places, helpful guidelines in dealing with a legal matter, and even something as simple as preparing a meal in twenty minutes or less.

Persons are often willing to pay on a per access basis or even a monthly subscription to have access to these types of sessions.

Selling this sort of service is not hard at all, once you identify the sectors of the population you wish to go after. Then it is a matter of securing the types of audio/video sessions that will click with your customers and making it easy for them to connect with the sessions.

Again, you may find it cost effective to partner with someone else, or it may be in the best interests of yourself and your customers to develop the sessions in house. You can evaluate your resources and make a sound decision on which way to go.

Mid ticket items are a great way to grab both a larger chunk of per unit profit, as well as create reliable revenue streams that you can depend on from month to month. Get some input from your existing customers and develop a nice suite of mid ticket offerings. You will be glad you did.

High Ticket Product Ideas

No suite of products or services is complete without some "diamond" level of offerings that are of interest to your customers.

While these may not appeal to more than a core group of your client base, the fact that you enjoy such a strong relationship based on the performance of your low ticket and mid ticket offerings will help them to trust you with these high ticket products as well.

When you think in terms of high ticket products and services, an average of $297.00 to $997.00 is a nice average range. Of course, there is nothing with going for high ticket products that are $1,000.00 or more, depending on how they relate to your other products and the demographics of your client base.

Here are some ideas for high ticket offerings that may be a great fit with your business model.

- **Coaching / Mentoring**

There is plenty of demand these days for professional coaches and motivational speaker. All across the country, people whose entire purpose is to inspire, instruct, and help people identify where they want to go in life are raking in very nice fees.

Motivational instructors and mentors are making their money with in person classes, but they are also doing very well with audio and visual sessions as well. Generally speaking, a class will be promoted and persons will be invited to register and pay a flat fee to attend.

Generally speaking, that fee will depend on the number of sessions that will be included in the series. Upon registration, the attendee will receive instructions on how to access the sessions via phone and/or the Internet.

The session will often allow for some degree of interaction, with the frequency and mode of interaction controlled by the mentor.

How does this relate back to your product line? Chances are you had to identify some specific applications for your offerings before you ever got your first sale. Some of your mentoring can be to help people understand how your other products save them time and money and in some cases help them to make more money and expand their business.

In a related note, if you have a number of customers who work in companies where dealing with customers is a daily thing, you can most certainly fill a void.

Among the mentoring sessions you could offer are such topics as how to defuse an angry customer, how to get a customer to tell you what is really bothering them and how to bring a former customer back into the fold.

You can draw on your own expertise as well as your experiences and come up with some motivational style mentoring classes that will be sure to be of interest to your customers.

- **Tele-Seminars**

Like mentoring sessions, tele-seminars are something that more and more people are comfortable with. They save time, definitely cut back on travel expenses, and allow attendees to get back to work more quickly, which helps to keep productivity high around the office.

When it comes to tele-seminars, you can offer subject matter you create and host in house, or you can become a means of providing a special guest speaker for a tele-seminar. Perhaps you can snag a bestselling author who has written an exciting new book on Internet marketing.

Arrange for a one time tele-seminar where the author discusses his book and entertains questions afterward. The audience will pay a flat fee to attend and have the ability to participate in the question and answer session. For additional revenue, you can make the proper arrangements to record the tele-seminar and make copies of it available after the fact.

• **Exclusive Membership Sites**

Everyone likes to feel special. One of the easiest ways is to create and manage an exclusive membership site. You can put together something that is specifically for a select group of persons, such as CEO's, chief financial officers, executive directors of non-profit organizations, or any niche market that is composed of people who could benefit from networking with their peers and can afford to pay a nice figure for that privilege on a monthly or annual basis.

Include in the membership discounts on items of interest such as trade magazines geared toward that market or savings on attended tele-seminars and mentoring sessions that are relevant to this exclusive group. By providing networking opportunities as well as the discounts, you can find yourself with a nice way to move high ticket offerings with no trouble at all.

• **Lucrative Service Such As Copywriting**

Support services are something that will always make an impact with businesses. By offering to take over such tasks as writing copy for new ad campaigns or sales and marketing collateral, preparing brochures, and editing other basic types of correspondence that the company uses regularly, you can save them a bundle and make a nice bit of profit for yourself.

Here are some reasons why outsourcing to you would be advantageous, rather than keeping it all in house:

- They do not have to pay your taxes. You are not an employee, so Payroll does not have to keep up with you.

- There are no perks such as insurance, retirement, or vacation to calculate. Working essentially as a consultant, none of these factors enter into the picture. They save money.

- The company can focus on its business without devoting a lot of resources to ancillary matters. You are dealing with all that.

- No time spent in development. They simply have to approve the finished product.

While it is true that consulting does not come cheap, it still ends up being much more cost effective than keeping someone on the payroll. Between the salary and the benefits that would be required by someone talented enough to do what you are offering to provide, you could be talking about saving tens of thousands of dollars over the course of a year.

The fact is that you can make quite a tidy profit by pitching a deal that requires an opt-in payment up front, with several smaller payments as each of the action items or projects are completed. This means some immediate profit for you, with the promise of more as the tasks are finished.

When it comes to providing high ticket offerings, knowing what your resources are and how well those match up with needs within your client base will help lead you to that type of high ticket products you can provide immediately, as well as help you prepare a laundry list of others that you hope to have set up and working in a short time.

CHAPTER 3- WHAT PROFIT STRATEGY SHOULD YOU EMPLOY?

When it comes to developing your ideal profit strategy, there are several things you can learn from the basic Profit Funnel. Let's take a look at those elementary principles:

Start from Scratch

Getting your foot in the door with a new customer is your top priority. We all know that they sales cycle can take a long time in some cases. But if you are going with a product or service that is relatively inexpensive and can be identified immediately with a need, then you can shorten than cycle a great deal.

Don't worry about making a huge profit off that first sale. Just get the sale and make sure the product works right. Your reputation and your future opportunities with that client rest on providing them with a quality product as a price they are happy with.

It is for that reason that these entry-level efforts are so important. Sure, the big profit is not there, although you may end up with a nice amount of profit if you are able to move a product or service in bulk.

But make sure you see this as laying a foundation for things to come and not just the beginning and the end of your efforts with this customer. If you handle the situation right, you will soon be in a position to make a great deal more inroads with this customer.

Don't Wait for New Opportunities to Find You

Now that you have a satisfied customer who likes what he has bought and now has a reason to trust you, the time has come to look for other ways to broaden your business dealings with your client. Identify mid-level products that you can offer to your customer, helping him to get ideas about how and where in the organization they may be effective.

Let your now excellent reputation precede you as you offer enhanced services that work with the original product offering, as well as more upscale services and products that can meet other needs within that company.

Keep in mind that as you expand your presence among various contacts associated with your main contact, there will be additional opportunities to begin the same process as outlined by the Profit Funnel with them. In addition, you will find that your clients are more than happy to act as references for you once you have provided them with multiple offerings that are doing a great job for them.

Learn the Trends to Anticipate Even the Most Infrequent Needs

You may have some high level services or products that will make a great impact on something your customer does once or twice a year. This is where your rapport with your client has come in handy. You know about these opportunities because you are trusted.

As you become aware of these chances to get involved with your high level offerings, make sure to demonstrate the value that you bring to the table. It is not just that you can save them more money, and most likely in these cases a great deal of money. You also can offer them at least as good and most likely better, than they have made do with in times past.

Keep in mind that though these high ticket chances may not come your way every month, the fact is that people remember when you had a hand in making them shine to their constituency at a critical moment.

Thus, if you offered consulting services that helped your client organize a successful week-long conference with persons coming from all fifty states to attend, your client will remember you very fondly and you will no doubt be called upon to provide those same services next year.

Deliver and Over-Deliver

Always keep in mind that all the goodwill that you have built up as you moved through the low ticket to mid ticket and finally high ticket offerings can be blown completely away with one simple failure to deliver what you promised.

There used to be a saying in the movie industry about a director – he was only as good as his last picture. That is also often the case with vendors who supply goods and services as well.

You can avoid disappointing your clients by making sure you do not promise them anything that cannot be delivered immediately. Far too often, salespersons say, "yes, we can do that" knowing full well there is nothing in place currently to deliver.

The result is that those that are backing you may or may not be able to come up with a solution. If they can't you have torpedoed your reputation with your customer, destroyed any hope of getting good word of mouth that could have opened doors for you elsewhere, and probably damaged the reputation of your company right along with your personal reputation.

Be honest about what you can provide and stay away from promising that which you know you don't have in place right now.

The concept of the Profit Funnel provides a common sense approach to selling. You start at this point and continue to build on that success. But don't get the idea that you take one company through the funnel and you are done with them. Over and over again, you can use the Profit Funnel to create new contacts within an existing client, perhaps at different locations or different departments.

You may even be at several points simultaneously with one single contact, as you identify more and more opportunities within the realm of his authority. By keeping the model of the Profit Funnel in mind, you will never find yourself in the rut of going only after the lowest hanging fruit on the tree.

You will scoop up that fruit of course. But you will also continue to reach upward as you progress from one level to the next, maximizing the time and assets of your customer, making a profit for your company, and getting an ever nicer commission for yourself.

In the end, you are in complete control of developing your persona ideal profit strategy. No matter what your product or service offerings, chances are they fit the mode of the Profit Funnel. Incorporate the concept into your profit strategy and use the Funnel as a way to measure your current level of success.

You will find it an excellent tool for helping you to stay on track as you reach for your goals.

CHAPTER 4- BOOST SALES WITH QUALITY INFORMATION

Insider Information

Every super affiliate is equipped with important tools and resources that help them set up shop quickly, whenever an upcoming launch is announced. These tools are invaluable to affiliates because we need to know when there is buzz building up around an upcoming launch BEFORE the majority of the public ever finds out about it.

The easiest way to make money with big launches is to have your system in place weeks before the launch actually happens. That way, you not only position yourself in the search engines for when the big day comes, but you're given enough time to create "value enhancers" that will draw customers to you, rather than the competition.

Maximize Your Investments!

One of these important tools is JV Notification. When you subscribe to a JV or launch notification program, you'll receive emails and updates about upcoming product launches long before the information is made available to potential customers. In fact, many times, you'll find out about upcoming product launches long before the merchant even begins to contact their own affiliates!

Consider how valuable this information is. When you know about upcoming launches in advance, you can secure web properties, build lists, set up Squeeze Pages, and even create bonus products that add value to the offer, AND you can start preparing your material well in advance, so that you have time to fine-tune your system before launch day.

Say "Act!"

Once you have a domain and website up and running, it's time to work on plugging in quality, informative and relevant content that will help potential customers make the decision to purchase the product through your affiliate link. Reviews need to be written so that they demonstrate to potential customers that you have personally evaluated the product, and have experience using the material.

Potential customers don't want to read reviews from affiliates, when they believe that the only reason you are recommending a product, is because you will earn a commission from doing so. While you always want to be transparent and comply with FTC regulations that stipulate that your visitors must be informed that you are compensated for any purchases made - you can still position yourself as an honest and reliable source of information by creating full featured reviews that highlight both the pros and cons of purchasing and using the product.

The best, most successful reviews are always written from a customer's perspective. They're designed to communicate directly with potential customers by getting into their frame of mind, and addressing the questions and concerns that they have. This means that you need to know your market! When you understand your market, you will be able to create compelling reviews and information pages that clearly address any potential concerns, and when you do that, you lower the wall of resistance, and are able to create high converting affiliate campaigns. When creating your website prior to launch, you'll want to evaluate the product so you can write detailed descriptions and reviews about the upcoming launch.

Give people a unique perspective on the product; let them know how you truly feel about the product, and whether the brand promise is fulfilled. You never want to promote products that you haven't evaluated, or that you don't feel will live up to the buyer's expectations.

Remember, every product you promote reflects your brand ethic, and demonstrates to customers whether you have their best interests at heart, so be cautious when promoting high-ticket items. You want to push people towards products that will ultimately help them achieve their goals, so that they will purchase through your campaign again, in the future. Set yourself apart, by focusing on promoting products from honest, experienced, and reputable sellers. Your customers will thank you for it!

CHAPTER 5- USING WEB SEO

Keyword Driven Domain

When it comes to cashing in on commissions from big launches, your domain name means everything. You want your domain to be keyword based, so that you can quickly rank in the search engines and "be found" by those desperately searching for more information about the product before, and during launch.

The key is to purchase a domain that is close to the product title, or website URL of the main launch. For added value, consider registering a domain name that includes keywords such as "bonus", "truth", "review", or perhaps "overview".

Examples:

ProductNameReview.com

ProductNameTruth.com

ProductNameBonus.com

And don't overlook domains with hyphens that break up the keywords, such as:

Product-Name-Review.com

Product-Name-Bonuses.com

When registering domain names to promote upcoming launches, you want to make sure that you are compliant with any rules or restrictions set out by the merchant. You want to develop a professional relationship with those you promote, and to share their products with the market in a way that reflects well on your brand. Don't use misleading tactics or questionable methods to promote affiliate campaigns because not only will it damage your relationships with those you promote, it will ultimately affect your credibility with your customers.

Optimized Website

When launch day takes place, customers will receive notice through email campaigns and lists that they have signed up to receive. However, the majority of customers won't purchase directly through email. In fact, most people feel that they need more information before making an informed decision as to whether they should purchase the product.

This is where you come in.

You want to build a website that is positioned within the search engines top results, so that people considering the product can find your website, explore your information, and eventually, purchase through your affiliate link.

Maximize Your Investments!

One of the easiest ways to convince potential customers to follow through on a purchase is to provide them with valuable and detailed information about the product. You can set up a website in a number of different ways, but the fastest and most cost effective strategy is to install a copy of WordPress, and then write detailed reviews and descriptions about what the product has to offer. The more information you provide, the better your chances at securing the sale. The great thing about WordPress, is that even if you lack experience creating websites, or you don't have a technical bone in your body, you will still be able to create highly optimized webpages quickly just by taking advantage of the built-in optimizer tools and free themes.

To enhance your website and further optimize your site for the search engines, you can plug in additional components, known as "plugins" that will make it even easier to gain top search engine rankings.

Here are the top plugins used by seasoned affiliate marketers:

All in One SEO Plugin

This plugin makes it easy to optimize every page on your WordPress blog for top search engine rankings! You can define Meta tag information, add keywords & descriptions, and customize your website right down to defining "no index" for pages and archives!

Google XML Sitemaps

This plugin will allow search engine spiders and crawlers to quickly index and archive your website pages, providing better positioning and overall tracking of new posts, pages and content!

Awesome Slider

This plugin provides an exceptionally awesome feature for grabbing those all-important, "money is in the list", emails addresses! This tool also makes it easier to create a clean looking website, by providing a super cool slide-in opt-in form that you can add to your WordPress site without taking up space! In addition, it looks so good that anyone visiting your site simply cannot ignore it, and it's free! This plugin also comes with full and easy to follow instructions for installation of plugins, on WordPress sites!

What Makes a Web 2.0 Secure?

From the moment that you decide to promote an upcoming product launch, you'll want to secure as many Web 2.0 properties as possible. You want to create optimized web pages that all link back to your main website, or in the event you don't have a website of your own, create one main hub and have all additional feeder sites point to your main "money page".

The key to effectively using Web 2.0 properties is to boost your ranking within the search engines through keyword-optimized content. Since these Web 2.0 properties are considered authority sites, you'll gain immediate backlinks and "SEO juice" just by creating quality pages within these free community sites. The higher you rank in Google on launch day, the more money you'll make from direct commissions - it's as simple as that! You only need a handful of original, high quality articles focusing on the product or in the event you don't have enough information about the product, you can simply create articles around the subject matter.

For example: When I was promoting a training course on website flipping, instead of writing about the product that I hadn't yet evaluated, I hired a freelancer to write 10 articles focusing on new website flippers. This way, I could begin submitting content immediately to gain positioning within the search engines. As I later evaluated the product, I adjusted the content to better fit (and promote) the niche market. In many cases, you can leave your content as is, and just add your affiliate link to the page when it gets closer to launch day. Make sure you check out the affiliate program terms, so that you can identify whether you are credited for all future sales immediately (by a cookie set with each referred visit), or whether you are only credited for sales that take place within a specific time frame.

You also want to know whether the affiliate program is set up to credit the first referral, or whether another affiliate can override your referral in the event a potential customer who has clicked on your affiliate link later clicks on another. It's important that you are credited for all of your promotional work, and the majority of merchants will reward the "first referral" with the credit of the sale but make sure you verify this before setting up your campaigns. You might have come across a website where the affiliate instructed you to remove your cookies and clear your cache before clicking on their link. They do this so that in the event you were originally referred by another affiliate, that affiliate link is wiped out from your machine.

The only time this method should be used is in the event that you are offering a bonus to potential customers, and you want to make sure that they purchase through your affiliate link, otherwise play fair... If another affiliate has worked hard to secure a referral, don't swipe it from them!

CHAPTER 6- THE KILLER OFFER AND THE RESULTING MAILING LIST

THE Bonus

Are you looking to stand out from other affiliates promoting the same launch? You need a hot, irresistible bonus offer that will motivate them to purchase through your affiliate link! Bonus offers need to tie in directly with what is being offered. They need to be relevant, but more importantly, they need to extend the value of the purchase.

For example, your bonus offers should serve as auxiliary components to the main product. If you were promoting

Maximize Your Investments!

BloggingToTheBank.com (a fictitious example), you could offer bonus items that included WordPress themes, WordPress video tutorials, or maybe content packs that new bloggers could use to jumpstart their websites. Analyze the product you are promoting, and determine what is missing or lacking in the main product. Then, create your bonus product around that unfilled need or demand. When creating your bonus product, you don't have to develop it yourself.

You can minimize costs by using high quality private label content, or other types of content that allows for distribution. You can then create compilations from existing material, or develop extensive bundles, collections, and packages that fit with the product you are promoting. Mailing List You now have the basics and understand the importance of a keyword driven domain name, Web 2.0 properties, an optimized website, and a killer bonus. To tie it all together, the final step is to set up an autoresponder system so that you can capture leads and follow up with potential customers.

The Basics of List Building

Building a list using squeeze pages and incentive offers will ultimately make your job as an affiliate much easier. You will be able to get your message out to an instant audience of confirmed subscribers, and will be able to minimize your workload when promoting future offers!

List building is all about connecting with your target audience by offering them high quality information in exchange for their confirmed email opt-in. You simply set up a targeted squeeze page that illustrates the benefits of joining your list, produce an irresistible incentive offer, and convert those leads into sales. Email marketers collect leads by using a combination of squeeze pages and opt-in forms. These forms are generated by your autoresponder provider and are embedded into the HTML code of your squeeze page template or the easy Awesome Slider plugin.

Each time a visitor to your squeeze page enters in their name and email address, they are added to your mailing list database, and become an active subscriber of your newsletter. List building helps facilitate the process of converting subscribers into active customers, since once your prospect has been added to our mailing list; you are able to develop a relationship with them. This relationship will encourage sales, as well as repeat sales. This will make up the largest majority of your email marketing income!

When it comes to setting up a mailing list, you will want a professional autoresponder account. An autoresponder simply collects the information from every lead that enters in their name and email address, storing it in an online database that you can access through your autoresponder administration center. Autoresponders also deliver content automatically, allowing you to set-up pre-loaded campaigns, which will deliver content based on specific time frames or dates. This kind of system allows for complete automation, so you can build it once and let it run on autopilot!

Once you have created your autoresponder account, you will be able to generate "opt in code" which is then installed on a squeeze page. The opt-in code is a form that asks visitors to enter in their name and email address and when entered, it triggers your autoresponder account to send out a confirmation email. A potential lead clicks on the confirmation email, verifying their request to be "added" to your list and once clicked; they become an active and verified subscriber! Your squeeze page is where the magic happens. It is where visitors are converted into subscribers – giving you the opportunity to transform subscribers into customers and repeat buyers. This is where you are able to grow your business, your brand, and your authority in every niche market you choose, it is the springboard to every product launch, and ultimately, the center point of your entire online business. The building of targeted mailing lists is such an integral part to the success of your online business; your squeeze page will serve as the entry point of your sales funnel. Therefore, you need to push them through the doorway into your backend system. Your incentive offer is the primary 'pull' that will motivate visitors into giving up their name and email address in exchange for access to your special offer, however, your squeeze page needs to be designed to showcase and highlight the benefits of being a subscriber.

To begin with, your squeeze page needs to be clean and free of clutter. You want visitors to focus on filling out the opt-in form generated by your autoresponder account. This means that you would need to take a very different approach to constructing your squeeze page, than in constructing a traditional sales page.

Your squeeze page should include:

1) Captivating headline and sub headline

2) Bullet list detailing the benefits of joining your list

3) High quality, targeted incentive offer

4) Opt in box, clearly identified on the page (preferably above the fold)

5) Privacy statement

6) Your name and contact information

That's it! You don't want a squeeze page that is graphic intensive, slow loading, complicated or confusing. You want to eliminate external links or navigation menus so that the ONLY option visitors have on this page, is to subscribe to your mailing list!

CHAPTER 7- HOW TO KEEP LIST BUILDING A LEGAL TACTIC

To begin, if you are just starting out in list building and you aren't quite set up yet, you'll need a handful of tools that will essentially, form the foundation of your complete email marketing system. The first thing you'll need is a professional autoresponder account.

Autoresponder services allow anyone to collect leads, while giving them the opportunity to categorize and organize all contacts so that you're able to segment your emails, split test campaigns and communicate with your target audience any time you wish. In fact, autoresponder systems will give you the option of setting up "preloaded" campaigns, which push out a sequence of emails automatically, each time a new subscriber joins your list.

For example, if you create an autoresponder sequence that contains 5 follow up emails, you can assign each one to go out on a specific date, OR after a subscriber has been a list member for a specific period of time. What this means is that you can literally create a complete autopilot email marketing system that connects with your subscribers, develops an ongoing relationship with your list and ultimately makes you money even when you are miles away from your computer! Now, we'll be honest with you – setting up your autoresponder sequences are often the most time consuming part of email marketing. You have to create enough content to sustain your list. After all, if you fail to stay in touch with your subscribers and to connect with them on a regular basis, all of your effort will be for naught – and your list will turn cold.

When your list turns cold, you're forced into re-building those relationships all over again because your subscribers have either forgotten all about you, or they won't feel as though you've offered enough value for them to remain active members. Either way, failing to follow up with your subscribers on a regular basis will cost you money. But it doesn't have to be so time consuming, or difficult. In fact, there is one resource available to you right now that will instantly solve the problem, making it easier than ever to develop high performance email campaigns by delivering hardcore value to your subscriber base.

High Powered Traffic Strategies

Once you've set up your squeeze page, created your autoresponder account and you have a combination of high quality content as well as an incentive offer available to new subscribers,

Maximize Your Investments!

it's time to start funneling in traffic to your squeeze pages, so you can begin capturing leads!

To begin, you should recognize that there are 3 traffic "tiers" that include:

- Partnering Traffic

- Customer Traffic

- Search Engine Traffic

With Partnering Traffic, the majority of your traffic will come from networking within your niche market. Now, this doesn't mean that you need to form joint ventures or alliances with anyone in your market, but it does mean that you can siphon traffic from competing websites, blogs, forums and even social media sites that focus on your chosen niche. Customer traffic is where you market directly to an existing customer base. If you've already managed to generate customers from other websites, or you've been involved in affiliate marketing or product development, the best way to start building a list is by targeting active buyers.

Search engine traffic consists of leads that come directly from the major search engines. This is organic, free traffic that lands on your squeeze pages because they've either been directed there after typing in relevant keywords, or they've followed incoming links from other websites that lead to your squeeze page. It's important that you focus on driving traffic to your squeeze pages from as many of these tiers as possible, so that you're able to maximize your opt-in rates. If you don't have an existing customer base, focus instead on traffic tier 1 and 3, piggybacking off of existing competitor blogs and forums, and in positioning your squeeze page so that it ranks within the search engines.

Here are a few quick and easy ways to do this:

Forum & Community Traffic

If you want to exploit the success of other websites in your market so that you're able to siphon traffic to your own squeeze page, one of the easiest ways to do this is via forum and community marketing. Think about it. What better way to get in direct contact with your customer base than with active community forums that focus specifically on your niche? It's like fishing in a bathtub! The first step is to create a resource list of relevant forums in your market, focusing only on active forums that carry a medium to high level of subscribers. Start-up forums are good for generating backlinks to your squeeze page, but if you want to really drive in subscribers, you'll want to spend your time being visible in high active community sites.

Forum marketing is one of the best ways of quickly jump-starting activity to your squeeze page, but forums are incredibly useful in many other ways as well, including:

•Quick & Easy Market Research

•Valuable FREE Feedback for your products

•Establishing a recognized brand as an authority in your market

•Generating quality backlinks to your squeeze page

•Get your website indexed faster than ever before

When it comes to finding forums in your market, you can browse through Google by entering in relevant keyword strings such as "yourniche+ forums" or "community forums+keyword", or you can take a look through forum directory sites. The key is to set up a complete profile so that your website URL is located both in your forum signature, AND in your profile.

Search Engine Marketing

Gone are the days where you could throw up a pay per click marketing campaign and instantly funnel in thousands of qualified leads. These days, it's all about "content marketing". You need to provide exceptional content to your market, and do your job at warming up potential subscribers so that they're motivated into joining your list. Thankfully, if you do your job at providing real value to potential subscribers, it's actually quite easy to generate insane traffic from search engines like Google.com, Yahoo.com or Bing. One way of maximizing traffic through the search engines is by exploiting the power of "authority websites" like Squidoo, Blogger, WordPress and HubPages. All of these websites are considered authority sites in the major search engines and so by having a webpage hosted with these networks, you'll be able to siphon 'link juice' to your squeeze pages, while giving your website an instant boost in the search engines.

You can piggyback off of these authority websites by setting up a simple website with each service. Here's a quick way to do it:

1: Set up a keyword-based domain. You want to make sure that your URL contains your most relevant keywords, so that you're able to generate immediate traffic to your site.

2: Set up a Squidoo lens, integrating various modules and content. You'll need 2-3 short articles in order to build a quality lens. Make sure that your content is unique and offers real value. Consider creating a tutorial style Squidoo lens, as they tend to rank even higher.

3: Set up a HubPages account and repeat the same steps that you took to create your Squidoo account. You can use the same content across both networks.

4: Now it's time to add in your opt-in box. With Blogger.com and Wordpress.com, you can copy and paste your squeeze page HTML directly into your new blog page. Test out your opt-in form making sure it works properly, and save your progress. You can also add modules to the sidebar of your Blogger and WordPress theme that house your opt-in code so that it's visible on every page of your site.

5: Add your opt-in code into your Squidoo lens, HubPages and both profile pages. You want to make sure to copy and paste your squeeze page opt-in box code only – not the entire squeeze page HTML as it won't display correctly. You can do this easily by adding in a "text module" to both your Squidoo lens and your Hubs.

Once you've set up this list building system, just rinse and repeat for every niche market that you are targeting. In fact, we've experienced a tremendous influx of subscribers just by creating simple websites with all authority sites, and best of all, once you've set them up, you never have to touch them again!

Keep in mind that you want to incorporate relevant keywords into the content you use on authority websites, so that you are able to generate traffic from the major search engines. Keywords form the connection between your marketing message and your target audience. The problem is, the majority of online marketers either don't know how to find quality keywords, or they go about it all the wrong way. You want to focus on BUYER keywords, because not only will it be easier to build a customer list of loyal buyers, but also it will be incredibly easy to maximize your income, because these people are ready to buy! The easiest way to choose the perfect keywords is to focus on specific keyword phrases.

The more targeted the keyword is, the more targeted your traffic; it's as simple as that. Google's free keyword tool that was released in 2007 takes the guesswork out of researching targeted keywords and instantly reveals the best keywords for virtually any market imaginable.

Social Media Marketing

Think of the methods that you currently use to target your niche market and communicate with potential customers, and then use those outlets to funnel traffic to your squeeze pages. For example, if you are active on Facebook, Twitter of Google+, you can easily create content around your market and lead your followers through to your squeeze page Consider adding your primary website, or squeeze page URL to all of your social media accounts, especially your profile page. You'll be surprised at just how much traffic you're able to generate just by taking advantage of the communication channels that you already use to target your market.

Increase Your Website's Buying Traffic

In order to make money in email marketing, you need to work consistently at generating traffic to your squeeze pages. You want to maximize your opt-in rates, and skyrocket your income by funneling in new business each and every day.

Here are a few quick ways to maximize your traffic, and your profits:

Create Multiple Squeeze Pages

You never want to stick to just one squeeze page, but instead, work towards building a complete network of squeeze and landing pages that target various markets. Even if you're only interested in one main niche, you should still create multiple squeeze pages that offer various incentives so that you can split-test your campaigns and determine what works, and what doesn't. Your goal should be to set up 2 squeeze pages a month, and then work consistently to funnel qualified traffic to each squeeze page, so that you're always adding new subscribers into your sales funnel.

Expand Your Outreach Every Month

Don't be afraid to branch out and expand your list building system. The more squeeze pages you have in circulation, the better. Test out different incentive offers, tweak your sales page copy and continue adding new email sequences into your autoresponder system so that you're in constant contact with your subscriber base. You also want to make sure that you're offering a series of both free and promotional based campaigns so that you're able to provide true value to your subscriber base, while monetizing your emails. You can do this by offering a free report, or a series of articles while mixing in promotional campaigns, affiliate links or announcements of your own product releases.

Split Test Your Squeeze Pages & Campaigns

Split testing squeeze pages is an important part of email marketing, because there is no way that you will be able to accurately predict how well your visitors will respond to your offer, without comparatively testing alternative layouts and incentive offers. One easy method of testing your pages and evaluating conversion rates is by using Google's Website Optimizer, a free tool that will help you run simple split tests of any websites you own.

Segment Your Lists

By segmenting your lists, you can create content based on each groups' interests and skill levels as well as develop products and services around each category of subscribers. This will ultimately maximize your income because you're no longer lumping all of your subscribers together, but instead, you're able to create specific email campaigns around what they have demonstrated interest in!

Stay Active

One of the biggest mistakes that new email marketers make is that they set up their email campaigns and let them run on complete autopilot. We're all about automating our business and email marketing CAN be automated to some degree; however you need to make sure that your email sequence is set to deliver content regularly. You NEED to stay in communication with each and every subscriber you have. To do this, try to set up every email campaign so that it contains enough content, spread out across several months.

For example, create 1 campaign that contains 30 articles and rather than sending out a new article each day, send out one article every week so that your content is spread out over time. Then, add in new content in between delivery cycles as often as possible so that in the end, your subscribers receive 1-2 new emails a week.

These emails should offer value in the form of free content or material. Next, choose to either integrate monetized content in between your free content delivery, or use the "broadcast" feature from within your Aweber account to send out immediate emails to your subscribers. Broadcasts are sent out only once, so if you want real automation, you'll want to schedule monetized content once or twice a week, combined with free content that offers access to valuable tools and information.

Do your best to offer an even balance of free and monetized content, so that your subscribers see the true value of remaining on your list. Setting up your email campaigns so that they push out regular broadcasts and emails does more for you than just making sure your lists don't run cold. When you develop a consistent pattern for communicating with your lists, your subscribers will be conditioned to expect emails on certain days, which will increase your open-rates dramatically!

ABOUT THE AUTHOR

Betty Wright is an investment strategist known for her valuable contribution to the success of most of the Fortune 500 companies. She is a graduate of Economics from the Harvard University with additional Master's Degree in Business and Finance.

Betty was the first in her family to attend college. Her parents sacrificed their farm just so she can graduate. According to parents Sally and Don Wright, their sacrifices paid off when Betty graduated at the top of her class and went on to build a strong reputation in the industry.

Today, Betty is a proud mom to Justin.

www.ingramcontent.com/pod-product-compliance
Lightning Source LLC
Chambersburg PA
CBHW051250170526
45165CB00004B/1658